Bibliographic information published by the German National Library:

The German National Library lists this publication in the National Bibliography; detailed bibliographic data are available on the Internet at http://dnb.dnb.de .

Imprint:

Copyright © 2018 GRIN Verlag
Print and binding: Books on Demand GmbH, Norderstedt Germany
ISBN: 9783346079046

This book at GRIN:

https://www.grin.com/document/510903

Carolina Gerwin

Justice according to Cicero. How is it to be upheld in the republic?

GRIN Verlag

GRIN - Your knowledge has value

Since its foundation in 1998, GRIN has specialized in publishing academic texts by students, college teachers and other academics as e-book and printed book. The website www.grin.com is an ideal platform for presenting term papers, final papers, scientific essays, dissertations and specialist books.

Visit us on the internet:

http://www.grin.com/

http://www.facebook.com/grincom

http://www.twitter.com/grin_com

What is justice, according to Cicero, and how is it to be upheld in the republic?

Carolina Gerwin

Marcus Tullius Cicero (106- 43 BC) is one of the most famous philosophical and political figures in the world. He has written several influential works such as *On Duties*, which has been seen as a "source of moral authority" since its publication in 44 BC. [1] Several scholars have analysed Cicero's works to understand and evaluate his political and philosophical ideas, also regarding Cicero's view on one of his key concepts: justice. This essay complements current literature by discussing what justice is, according to Cicero, and how it is preserved in the republic. I argue that for the philosopher, justice is the superior virtue among all people that prevails over other virtues and promotes sociability, thereby upholding the community and the state. Justice is upheld in the republic if everyone acts according to certain rules that are outlined below and if power is divided between the monarchic, aristocratic and democratic elements in Cicero's account of a mixed constitution. The essay starts by explaining the relevant context, then continues by outlining Cicero's view on justice, and finally, it discusses how it is preserved in the republic as described in *On the Commonwealth* and *On Duties*.

Writing *On the Commonwealth* (54- 51 BC), Cicero aimed at two points: He wanted to outline the characteristics of the best constitution but, more importantly, he sought to "determine how the Roman state can be prevented from collapsing under the present strain of disunity".[2] The reason for this is that the Roman republic suffered under factionalism because, as pointed out by Laelius in Cicero's *On the Commonwealth*, due to the demise of Tiberius Gracchus and his tribunate, 'there are two senates and almost two peoples' (1.31). During Cicero's times, there was an ideological struggle between the 'populares' and 'optimates': The former view is associated with Caesar and the Gracci brothers, while Cicero had "overtly republican optimate preferences."[3] According to Laelius, if unity was achieved again, 'then we will live both better and happier lives' (*On the Commonwealth* 1.32). As *On Duties* complements *On the Commonwealth*, it serves the same purpose, probably even more: After Cicero's return from exile in 57 BC, the triumvirate between Pompey, Caesar and Crassus was renewed and although Cicero opposed the alliance, he had to bent down for the sake of the stability

---

[1] Benjamin Patrick Newton, "Introduction," in *On Duties* by Marcus Tullius Cicero, translated and edited by B.P. Newton (Ithaca and London: Cornell University Press, 2016), 1.

[2] Elizabeth Asmis, "The State as a Partnership: Cicero's Definition of "res publica" in his work "On the State"," *History of Political Thought* 25 (Winter 2004): 572.

[3] E.M. Atkins, "'Domina et regina virtutum': Justice and Societas in "De Officiis"," *Phronesis* 35 (1990): 281.

of the Republic and his own life.[4] Consequently, although he already recognised in 54 BC that the Republic is divided and reigned by "individuals exercising power for their own good", he did not take action but rather preferred to express his opinion by writing texts such as *On the Commonwealth*.[5] As reasonably pointed out by Asmis, his apprehension to give offense against Pompey and Caesar is probably the reason why Cicero used Scipio in *On the Commonwealth* to express his views.[6] After the death of Crassus in 53 BC, the triumvirate collapsed and the following competition between Caesar and Pompey culminated in the beginning of a civil war in 49 BC after Caesar had crossed the Rubicon.[7] Cicero himself supported Pompey but remained more or less inactive during the war.[8] Finally, Caesar became the dictator of Rome in 49 BC and once more, Cicero "turned to study as a profitable way of spending his time and consoling himself for the loss of the *res publica*".[9] However, after the assassination of Caesar in 44 BC, Cicero's view on his writing changed and his philosophical works become much more political.[10] Consequently, as Long puts it, *On Duties* is also written as an "attack on the perversion" of the 'mos maiorum' by Caesar[11] in order to accuse him as the "Republic's destroyer".[12] Therefore, regarding Cicero's view on justice, the crisis of the republic, provoked by factionalism, tyranny and Caesar's death, had a major influence . Consequently, to prevent the collapse of the Roman Republic and to re-establish its stability, the author suggests in *On Duties* to persuade the rulers of the Republic to govern according to duties that reflect both honesty (in accordance with virtues such as justice) and usefulness because 'whatever is honourable is beneficial' (*On Duties* 3.35).

Regarding the question what justice is, it is important to understand Cicero's account of humanity. Cicero begins his reflection of the roots of human society with a "general account of animal *oikeiosis*", which can be translated as an instinct for sociability, and uses therefore the "properly ethical approach" to justice[13]: In *On Duties* 1.11, Cicero explains that every creature has a drive for self-preservation, an urge for procreation and a 'certain care' for new-borns. In contrast to animals,

---

[4] Elizabeth Asmis, "A New Kind of Model: Cicero's Roman Constitution in "De republica"," *American Journal of Philology* 126 (Autumn 2005): 386-87.
[5] Asmis, „A New Kind of Model," 387.
[6] Ibid., 391.
[7] E.M. Atkins, "Cicero," in *The Cambridge History of Greek and Roman Political Thought,* edited by C. Rowe and M. Schofield (Cambridge: Cambridge University Press, 2000), 502.
[8] Atkins, "Cicero," 502-03.
[9] Ibid., 503.
[10] Ibid., 504.
[11] A.A. Long, "Cicero's Politics in "De Officiis"," in *Justice and Generosity,* edited by Laks & Schofield (1995) [repr.in his *From Epicurus to Epictetus: Studies in Hellenistic and Roman Philosophy* (2006)], 215.
[12] Long, "Cicero's Politics in "De Officiis"," 219.
[13] Malcolm Schofield, "Two Stoic Approaches to justice," in *Justice and Generosity,* edited by Laks and Schofield (Cambridge: Cambridge University Press, 2009), 193-194.

humans have 'reason', creating a desire to unite with other humans for the 'fellowship of both common speech and of life, creating above all a particular love for his offspring' and the wish to share useful things with others (*On Duties* 1.12). This aspect is especially important for the creation and upholding of a community and, as we will see, for Cicero's view on justice. A second characteristic of humans is their 'search for truth and its investigation' (*On Duties* 1.13). Consequently, humans want to develop by getting new knowledge to live a pleasant life by recognising that 'what is true, simple and pure' is most natural to humans (*On Duties* 1.13). Furthermore, this characteristic is associated with an 'impulse towards pre-eminence', resulting in the wish to only be ruled by a leader legitimate and just, in a '(g)reatness of spirit' and a disdain for human concerns (*On Duties* 1.13). While the former points are crucial for making a society possible, the last two points show the tendencies for conflict, reflected in the crisis of the Roman Republic as outlined in the beginning. However, our ability to digest our environment leads to the thinking that 'beauty, constancy and order should be preserved' in all aspects (*On Duties* 1.14) and counteracts such a potential for disputes. Therefore, "sociability" is the natural foundation of justice and humans consequently seek to live in the 'res publica'.[14] According to Cicero, justice is the consequence of our "innate instincts" and our "truly human desires" are those for justice,[15] implying that justice is natural to all humans.

Therefore, next to wisdom, courage, and temperance, justice is one of the four cardinal virtues (*On Duties* 1.15). As justice is 'the mistress and queen of all virtues' (*On Duties* 3.28), it is the most important virtue and most far-reaching source of duty, acting as the guardian of the state by preserving the drive for unity in every individual. Atkins' argument stresses this point by stating that the role of justice is the "building up of *societas*."[16] This is confirmed by the definition of justice in its broader perception, namely its "obligation to maintain human association", the main idea in Cicero's first book of *On Duties*.[17] However, one can also find a definition of justice in the "narrower sense" that is more similar to the "orthodox Stoic definition."[18] Justice is more explicitly defined as upholding the community 'with faithfulness to agreements one has made' and 'with assigning to each his own' (*On Duties* 1.15) by treating 'common goods as common and private ones as one's own' (*On Duties* 1.20). A further crucial part of justice is that 'no man should harm another unless he has been provoked by injustice' (*On Duties* 1.20). This definition of justice is significantly influenced by the crisis of the republic and Cicero's own experiences: He probably included the part about not hurting each other as he was a witness of the civil war, and from his time in exile follows his defence of

---

[14] Atkins, "'Domina et regina virtutum'," 281.
[15] Ibid., 288.
[16] Ibid., 266.
[17] Schofield, "Two Stoic Approaches to justice," 204.
[18] Ibid.

private property (*On Duties* 1.21), a point stressed several times in *On Duties* because according to the philosopher, the 'proper function of citizenship and a city' is to guarantee for all a 'free and unworried guardianship of his possessions' (2.78). Moreover, as the republic suffered under factionalism, the author stresses that in order 'to bind fast the fellowship of men with each other', it is just to share what has been given to people by nature and one should help each other (*On Duties* 1.22). Furthermore, two kinds of injustice follow from these points: To commit injury and to not prevent someone of inflicting an infringement (*On Duties* 1.23).

Therefore, in sum, the main elements of justice are to not hurt anyone and to act with regard to the common good (*On Duties* 1.31), as well as to prevent others from committing injustice. If everyone acts according to these rules, justice becomes the main driver for a stable and flourishing state because, as it is the most important human association that unites all that means something to us (*On Duties* 1.57), the republic becomes the main reference point of one's actions (*On Duties* 1. 58). As Cicero was a witness of the civil war beginning 49 BC between Caesar and Pompey, two men focusing on their own advantage and seeking to rule over the Republic,[19] it is understandable that in his theory of justice, the virtue has to establish a state where people and especially politicians care about other citizens and serve the common good rather than their own one.

In order to understand the political role of justice, according to the philosopher, it is crucial to understand its relationship to other virtues as it illustrates how justice functions. Regarding wisdom, justice limits our urge for the search and investigation of truth by making sure that one is not 'drawn by such a devotion away from practical achievements', which would be contrary to our duties (*On Duties* 1.19). This reason for this is that virtue needs to be expressed in deeds to be honourable (*On Duties* 1.19) and as wisdom's 'most important employment is the governance of states' (*On the Commonwealth* 1.2), it should be oriented to the benefit of the republic and should be followed by its application to enrich the life in the republic. Comparing justice with wisdom, Cicero stresses that wisdom should be about knowledge that concerns the human race, including the 'sociability and fellowship of gods and men with each other' (*On Duties* 1.153). And although the work of people who have dedicated their lives to the search and investigation of truth are beneficial for the state, the duties of justice which are oriented towards the 'benefit of mankind' are always superior (*On Duties* 1.155).

The same applies to courage: Cicero agrees with the Stoic definition of courage as 'the virtue that fights on behalf of fairness' (*On Duties* 1.62) and therefore, justice must be present in all actions that a great spirit does, making sure that deeds are done for the common good and the state and not for

---

[19] Atkins, "Cicero", 502.

one's own benefit (*On Duties* 1.62-63). The problem, however, is that as especially those who are of great spirit feel the desire to be pre-eminent and better than anyone else (*On Duties* 1.64), these people may desire to become the 'sole ruler' and use violent and unjust actions to reach their goals (*On Duties* 1.64). In this passage, Cicero attacks Caesar who competed with Pompey over the rule of Rome, which resulted in a civil war after he had crossed the Rubicon in 49 BC, and finally became the dictator of Rome.[20] To ensure the stability of the republic, justice therefore has to suppress the desire for pre-eminence and consequential false glory as only people who prevent others from causing injustice, one aspect of Cicero's definition of justice, are truly courageous and of great spirit (*On Duties* 1.65). According to the Roman thinker, true glory can be achieved through accomplishing the 'duties of justice' *(On Duties* 2.43) as the three means for glory, namely 'goodwill', 'faithfulness', and 'admiration' are all achieved through that one virtue: While the first two are aimed at the common good, the third one counteracts the wishes men are drawn to out of 'greed' (*On Duties* 2.38).

Regarding modesty and moderation, there might be situations where justice should not have precedence, as there are some deeds that a 'wise man would not do them even to protect his country' *(On Duties* 1.159). However, it is stressed that the fulfilment of such deeds would not benefit the republic (*On Duties* 1.159) and therefore, it is not an act against justice and the republic if sociability is not prioritised over other virtues. In 1.141 in *On Duties*, Cicero gives a summary of the last virtue and the duties that derive from it: The most important point is that 'impulse must obey reason' , the second is that one has to 'keep in mind the importance of the thing we wish to achieve' ensuring that we do not spend too much on it, and thirdly, 'we should be careful to moderate all things that may affect our appearance and standing as a gentleman'. Justice does play an indirect role here because especially regarding the first rule by assuring that one's actions are not controlled by our feelings but rather by rational thinking. If reason rules over our appetites, it is easier for us to recognise and to fulfil our duties as a statesman (*On Duties* 1.41), thereby ensuring the stability of the state. Furthermore, in general, moderation, seemliness and related virtues, especially if strengthened by justice and therefore oriented towards the benefit of the state, are in themselves already beneficial for the state, especially as the duty of seemliness is to behave in accordance with nature (*On Duties* 1.100), meaning that one's acts are made in favour of the community.

Due to these observations, I agree with Atkins in the point that justice is the most important of the four cardinal virtues and that it helps in defining them.[21] However, he argues that its role is to limit the other virtues[22] and while I agree that this is true for wisdom and courage, I believe that the role of

---

[20] Ibid., 502-503.
[21] Atkins, "'Domina et regina virtutum'," 258.
[22] Ibid., 258.

justice is not solely a limiting but also a supporting one. This can be (indirectly) seen in the case of the last virtue.

How is justice upheld in the republic, according to Cicero? The first reference point for an answer is taking a look at Cicero's definition of the state. He defines the commonwealth as 'the concern of a people, but a people is not any group of men assembled in any way, but an assemblage of some size associated with one another through agreement on law and community of interest' (*On the Commonwealth* 1.39a). Two points are standing out here: Firstly, by using the words 'concern of a people', Cicero stresses that the commonwealth is the possession of the people, implying that the folk should rule the state and not the other way around. Secondly, the nation consists of a group of people that is united in two ways, by the consensus on law and the solidarity of interests. It is worth to note here that Asmis argues that Cicero's view on the state is that of a "partnership"[23] and by using words such as "res publica, iuris consensu, utilitatis communione and sociatus" in his definition, which are all applicable to a partnership, this point is supported.[24] Regarding the origin of the state, the philosopher claims in *On the Commonwealth* that it is 'a kind of natural herding together of men' (1.39a) and mentions in 1.1 that 'nature has given men such a need for virtue and such a desire to defend the common safety'. Due to these points, one can see that it is important for Cicero that the state is based on harmony and stability, with people caring about each other and about the good of the state. As explained above, the political role of justice is prevailing over and controlling the other virtues to achieve such a community and to prevent the collapse of the Roman Republic.

Moreover, for upholding justice in the state, the constituency of the state plays a crucial role. In book 1 of *On the Commonwealth*, the constitutions of democracies, aristocracies and monarchies are analysed and Scipio comes to the conclusion that he prefers a mixed constitution that combines aspects from all of the three above-mentioned constitutions (1.45 and 1.54). The strength of Cicero's mixed constitution is that by combining the strength of a democracy, aristocracy and monarchy, the state remains firm.[25] Therefore, the mixed constitution has accordingly three elements: Scipio states that he accepts 'having something outstanding and monarchic in a commonwealth; of there being something else assigned to the authority of aristocrats; of some things being set aside for the judgment and wishes of the people' (*On the Commonwealth* 1.69). As suggested by Asmis, the "assignment of 'authority' (auctoritas) to the senate" makes Cicero's mixed constitution unique and implies that the magistrates or consuls, the monarchic element, and the people, the democratic element, are inferior

---

[23] Asmis, "The State as a Partnership," 569.
[24] Ibid., 580.
[25] Atkins, "Cicero," 491.

to the aristocratic factor of the constitution.[26] This can be seen in 1.41 in *On the Commonwealth*, when it is claimed that the Senate ensures the stability of the republic and must serve the 'original cause which engendered the state'. This means that the Senate as the most important body of the republic must foster the unity and virtues of Roman citizens. However, the people have a say in who is ruling by electing the members of the senate based on 'virtue and courage' (*On the Commonwealth* 1.51). According to Scipio (and therefore Cicero), this is the best solution for balancing the 'weakness of a single person and the rashness of many' and if the 'aristocrats look after the commonwealth then the populace is of necessity most blessed' (*On the Commonwealth* 1.52). The third element, the one of monarchy, is expressed through the power of the magistrates (*On the Commonwealth* 1.63). Cicero stresses that only when there is an 'equitable balance in the state of rights and duties and responsibilities, so that there is enough power in the hands of the magistrates and enough authority in the judgment of the aristocrats and enough freedom in the people' the stability of the republic can be ensured (2.57).

Focusing on justice, the author emphasizes its importance by stating that as long as a constitution 'holds to the bond which first bound men together in the association of a commonwealth', namely justice and usefulness, it is an acceptable way of ruling the state (*On the Commonwealth* 1.42). For Cicero, justice, as a crucial part of honesty, and utility are important for fulfilling one's obligations as a statesman, because, in order to prevent the collapse of the state, especially politicians have to rule according to duties that reflect both honesty and usefulness. However, neither a democracy, nor an autocracy nor a monarchy fulfil this condition according to Cicero (*On the Commonwealth* 1.43). But in his account of the mixed constitution, "the three key values or capacities necessary to the maintenance of justice and utility" are divided between three groups and the problem is solved[27]: According to Scipio, 'kings captivate us by their affection, aristocrats by their judgment, and the people by its liberty' (*On the Commonwealth* 1.55). While the monarchical element fills the gap of solidarity between the people and the elite through its affection, the aristocratic element is better than ordinary people in giving advice, and the people are better equipped in protecting liberty than the often corrupt elite.[28] This shows that for Cicero, it is important that power is distributed and a balance of powers is achieved that keep each other in check. Consequently, the stability of the state is secured, the monarch's power is limited to prevent the rise of a dictator such as Caesar, and harmony is achieved. Furthermore, the solidarity of the state is strengthened by the presence of a 'guide and helmsman' of the republic who is described as 'good and wise and knowledgeable about

---

[26] Asmis, "A New Kind of Model," 403-404.

[27] Xavier Marquez, "Cicero on the Stability of States," *History of Political Thought* 32 (Autumn 2011): 411.

[28] Marquez, "Cicero on the Stability of the States," 411-412.

the interests and the reputation of the state' and who 'can protect the state by his wisdom and effort' (*On the Commonwealth* 2.51). These statesmen are not only representatives of the senate, although they often belong to that social group, but are embodying the mixed constitution promoting harmoniousness between the democratic, aristocratic and monarchic groups of the republic.[29] One of the functions to reach this harmony is by actively employing and spreading virtue (*On the Commonwealth* 1.2). Therefore, in Cicero's account of the mixed constitution and the state, the conditions for stability and the promotion of justice and utility are given: Such as justice prevailing over our virtues, the guardians, mostly therefore the Senate, create solidarity between the three parts of the mixed constitution that ensure the distribution of power and consequently, all people can act and fulfil their duties according to utility and honesty, especially justice, and therefore on behalf of human kind and the republic.

In conclusion, as Cicero lived in an age with no political stability, where leaders such as Caesar cared about their own position rather than the whole republic, Cicero codifies political relationships through duties that have to reflect honesty (according to the four cardinal virtues) as well as utility. For Cicero, justice is the most important virtue, prevailing over our virtues and strengthening our sociability. It controls our virtues by reinforcing those that are beneficial for the common good and suppressing those that could endanger the stability of the state. For the philosopher, justice is defined as not hurting anyone and distinguishing between private and public interests and it is fundamental to it that one acts towards the common good and the stability of the state. According to Cicero, if people, especially politicians stick to these rules and fulfil their duties according to honesty, especially based on justice, as well as utility, and if power is divided as outlined in Cicero's account of the mixed constitution, justice (and utility) can be upheld in the state. In the context of the crisis of the Roman Republic, Cicero outlined these thoughts in *On Duties* and *On the Commonwealth* to re-establish the unity and stability of the state. But unfortunately, Cicero's goal had not been achieved and the Roman Republic collapsed shortly after Cicero's death.

---

[29] Asmis, "A New Kind of Model," 412.

Bibliography

Asmis, Elizabeth. "The State as a Partnership: Cicero's Definition of "res publica" in his work "On the State"." *History of Political Thought* 25 (Winter 2004): 569-98. https://www-jstor-org.libproxy.ucl.ac.uk/stable/pdf/26220253.pdf?refreqid=excelsior%3Ae18dab8fefca616ab1aac857 92aca1a5.

Asmis, Elizabeth. 2005. "A New Kind of Model: Cicero's Roman Constitution in "De republica"." *American Journal of Philology* 126 (Autumn): 377-416. https://www-jstor-org.libproxy.ucl.ac.uk/stable/pdf/3804937.pdf?refreqid=excelsior%3A051194078ef3295c59af48a9 72f61c62.

Atkins, E.M. 1990. "'Domina et regina virtutum': Justice and Societas in "De Officiis"." *Phronesis* 35: 258-89. https://www-jstor-org.libproxy.ucl.ac.uk/stable/pdf/4182365.pdf?refreqid=excelsior%3A73182db71ee9234d4e039e1a d365de28.

Atkins, E. M. 2000. "Cicero." In *The Cambridge History of Greek and Roman Political Thought,* edited by C. Rowe and M. Schofield, 477-516. Cambridge: Cambridge University Press. https://www.cambridge.org/core/services/aop-cambridge-core/content/view/0B616709BF8BC283B9FA6ABFE9611341/9781139053716c24_p477-516_CBO.pdf/cicero.pdf.

Cicero, Marcus Tullius. 1991. *On Duties.* Edited and translated by M.T. Griffin and E.M. Atkins. Cambridge: Cambridge University Press.

Cicero, Marcus Tullius. 1999. *On the Commonwealth and On the Laws.* Translated by. J. Zetzel. Cambridge: Cambridge University Press.

Long, A. A. 2006. "Cicero's Politics in "De Officiis"." In *Justice and Generosity,* edited by Laks & Schofield (1995) [repr.in his *From Epicurus to Epictetus: Studies in Hellenistic and Roman Philosophy* (2006)], 213-240. https://www.cambridge.org/core/services/aop-cambridge-core/content/view/2A9272C335CDD6468FF2B6782526E4B9/9780511518485c8_p213-240_CBO.pdf/ciceros_politics_in_de_officiis.pdf.

Marquez, Xavier. 2011. "Cicero on the Stability of States." *History of Political Thought* 32 (Autumn): 397-423. https://www-jstor-org.libproxy.ucl.ac.uk/stable/pdf/26225734.pdf?refreqid=excelsior%3Af45fd90753a756703e05269 4a4a247f8.

Newton, Benjamin Patrick. 2016. "Introduction." In *On Duties* by Marcus Tullius Cicero, translated and edited by B.P. Newton, 1-11. Ithaca and London: Cornell University Press. https://www-jstor-org.libproxy.ucl.ac.uk/stable/10.7591/j.ctt20d8b21.

Schofield, Malcolm. 2009. "Two Stoic Approaches to justice." In *Justice and Generosity,* edited by Laks and Schofield, 191-212. Cambridge: Cambridge University Press. https://www.cambridge.org/core/services/aop-cambridge-core/content/view/5AFF82BD6842479FB38015D1E7EF8AEC/9780511518485c7_p191-212_CBO.pdf/two_stoic_approaches_to_justice.pdf.

YOUR KNOWLEDGE HAS VALUE

- We will publish your bachelor's and
  master's thesis, essays and papers

- Your own eBook and book -
  sold worldwide in all relevant shops

- Earn money with each sale

Upload your text at www.GRIN.com
and publish for free